THE SMART KID'S GUIDE TO

Using the Internet

BY M. J. COSSON • ILLUSTRATED BY RONNIE ROONEY

Published by The Child's World®
1980 Lookout Drive • Mankato, MN 56003-1705
800-599-READ • www.childsworld.com

Acknowledgments
The Child's World®: Mary Berendes, Publishing Director
Content Adviser: Philip C. Rodkin, Professor of Child
Development, Departments of Educational Psychology and
Psychology, University of Illinois
The Design Lab: Design
Red Line Editorial: Editorial Direction
Amnet: Production

Photographs ©: Shutterstock Images, cover, 1, 6, 10, 13, 19,
20, 22, 25, 26, 27, 28, 29; Panom Pensawang/Shutterstock
Images, 5; Michael Jung/Shutterstock Images, 7; Tyler Olson/
Shutterstock Images, 9; Gladskikh Tatiana/Shutterstock Images,
12, 18; F. Jimenez Meca/Shutterstock Images, 14; Thinkstock,
15; Angela Waye/Shutterstock Images, 17

ISBN 9781626873476
LCCN 2014930686

Printed in the United States of America
Mankato, MN
July, 2014
PA02224

ABOUT THE AUTHOR

M. J. Cosson was born in Des Moines, Iowa. She has worked as a writer, teacher, editor, and artist. She lives in the Texas Hill country with her husband and pets.

ABOUT THE ILLUSTRATOR

Ronnie Rooney took art classes constantly as a child. She was always drawing and painting at her mom's kitchen table. She got her BFA in painting from the University of Massachusetts at Amherst and her MFA in illustration from the Savannah College of Art and Design in Savannah, Georgia. Ronnie lives on a U.S. Army base with her infantryman husband and two small children. Ronnie hopes to pass on her love of art and sports to her kids.

CONTENTS

CHAPTER 1
A Day on the Internet

What would you do without the Internet? You can live without the Internet. Most people have only been using the Internet since the 1990s. But we depend on the Internet more and more today.

You can find the answer to almost any question on the Internet. You can **communicate** with friends and family who are far away. You can find movies, music, and all kinds of entertainment, too. Maybe you use the Internet at school or the library. Maybe you use a computer at home. Or maybe you use a cell phone, tablet, or other mobile device. There are many ways to get online!

Some scientists think the Internet could be hurting our brains. We use it to find answers sometimes instead of thinking for ourselves. Others think the Internet is making us smarter. We can combine our creative thinking with the Internet's abilities. Think about how you use the Internet. How does the Internet help you be more creative? How does the Internet help us work together?

How does your family use the Internet?

Think about how you and your family use the Internet each day. Do the following activities sound familiar?

- Mom checks her online calendar to see what her plans are. She checks a **social networking site** for news about her friends and family.
- Dad checks the weather and the traffic report online.
- You get a text message from your best friend. You send your grandmother an e-mail with a photo from your birthday.
- You watch an online video about insect life cycles in class. Then the school librarian helps

you find a Web site to do research for your grasshoppers report.

- Your class holds a video chat with your pen pals in Ireland.
- You play a game on a cell phone after school.
- You listen to music or watch a movie on the Internet.
- Your parents buy something from an online store.

Look at this list. Think about how using the Internet helped. Did it make it easier to get information? Did it make learning more interesting? Did it make life go more smoothly? In what ways do you use the Internet?

People use the Internet at home, at school, at work, and at play.

CHAPTER 2
Smart Searching

The amount of information on the Internet is staggering. People around the world do millions of searches every minute. The Internet is a great place to learn things for school or for yourself.

You can do research for a report on the Internet. When you search on the Internet, use a kid-friendly **search engine**. Ask a teacher or librarian for his or her favorites. Another good source is an online **encyclopedia**. Your school has online encyclopedias. A teacher or librarian can help you find them.

You can also use online encyclopedias from home. However, sometimes you have to pay to use them. Or you can go to your local library.

The Internet offers many tools to help you learn, too. You can find how-to videos. There are programs and games for practicing math, reading, and other school subjects. There are Web sites that translate between languages. Some even read the words out loud. You can find many of these things using a search engine for kids. Or search with a teacher, parent, or other adult helping.

An adult can help you get the most out of the Internet.

You can't trust everything you read on the Internet.

You have to watch out on the Internet. Sometimes the information you see isn't trustworthy.

Look for Web sites that end in these letters:

.edu — a college or university

.gov — the U.S. government

They have more trustworthy information.

Sometimes you can find good information from these sites, too:

.com — a business, such as a magazine or newspaper

.org — a club or organization that might study your topic

Some Web sites end with other letters. They might not have reliable information. Read the information carefully. It might not be a reliable source if it sounds like someone's **opinion**.

Is the author's name on the Web site? Is there a date to show how old the information is? Is the site from someplace you have heard of, such as a museum? Are there links to other good sites? If you can answer yes to these questions, you probably have found a reliable Web site.

Use common sense when you read something online. Can you tell if the Web site is selling something? Does it want to **convince** you of something? Does it match what you already know about the subject? Can you find another good Web site that agrees?

There are millions of ways to entertain yourself online.

The Internet is also a great place to find entertainment. You can find movies, music, games, and more. When you search for entertainment, there are a few things you need to know first.

1. Make sure that it is okay to play a game online. Also make sure that an adult has approved your choice.

2. Wear headphones or earbuds if you are near others so you will not disturb them. Set the sound at a very low level. Loud noise coming through earbuds

can hurt your hearing. Many teenagers are losing their hearing because of loud music in their earbuds.

3. Listen to music on kid-friendly music sites. Use a kid-friendly search engine or ask an adult to help you find the song you want. Your family can also buy music files online.

4. There are many ways to find a movie to watch. Your family can pay to watch popular movies. Some movies and television shows are available online for free. You can also watch short videos online. An adult should check the rating of any show you want to watch.

The Internet makes learning fun, too!

When you do homework or write a report, keep track of where you found the information.

Some things are on the Internet for everyone to enjoy. Other things are on the Internet for people to buy. Things for sale could include music, books, art, movies, or other files. Don't copy something from the Internet that is for sale without paying for it. That's stealing. Ask your school media specialist if you are not sure about copying something.

Do not copy information, writing, or pictures and claim them as your own. This is called **plagiarism**.

It is okay to use an idea from someone else. But you need to rewrite it in your own words. It is usually okay to copy someone's writing or picture if you say whose it is. It is not okay to say you wrote it or made it.

Many schools have a space for books, computers, and electronic devices. Some schools call this a library or a media center. The person in charge might be called a school librarian or a media specialist. He or she can answer any questions you have about research, books, or the Internet.

CHAPTER 3

Staying in Touch

There are many ways you can use the Internet to communicate. E-mail is a great way to keep in touch. An e-mail can be like a conversation. You can write to one person or many people at a time. You can attach a photo or video to an e-mail, too.

Video chatting lets you see and talk with friends and relatives. One site many people use is Skype. You can show your grandma your loose tooth. You can show your friend a close-up of your yucky skinned

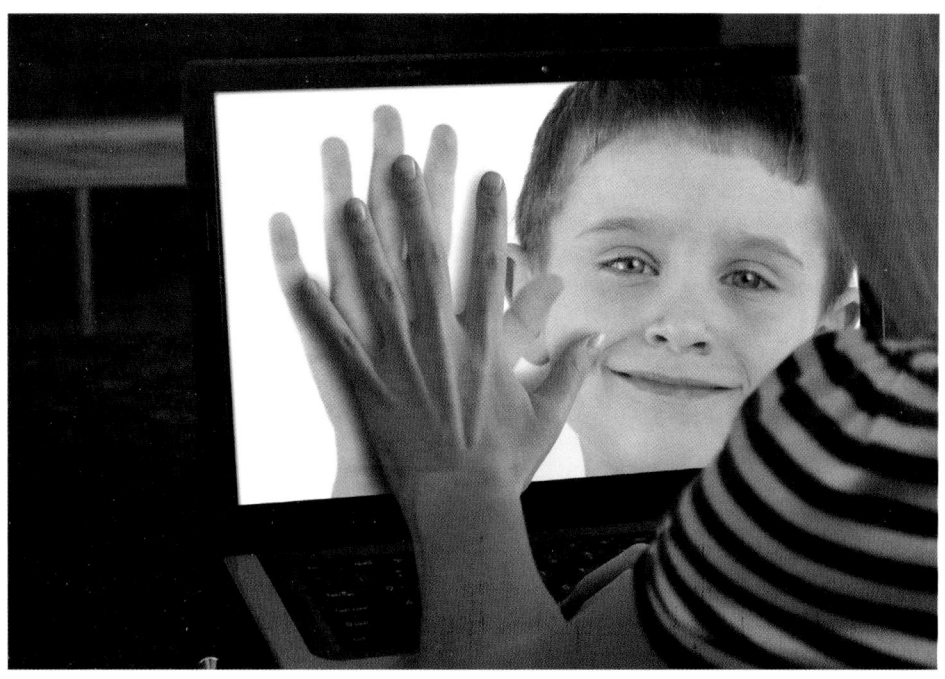

Video chatting can help when people miss friends or family members who are far away.

knee. You can aim the camera toward your dog or show your aunt your latest artwork.

Spam is junk e-mail. It comes from people or businesses you don't know. You need to delete it if you have an e-mail account. Only open e-mails from people you trust. If an e-mail from a friend seems weird, don't open it or click any links. The e-mail might not really be from them. Their account could have been **hacked**. Ask an adult before you open e-mail attachments. They could have a computer **virus**.

A webcam connected to a computer is one way to make online videos.

The Internet is all about sharing, too. It is fun to watch videos online and make your own videos. Many smartphones have video cameras. There are many sites where you can edit a video. You can post the video online. Have an adult help you.

Facebook and Twitter are just two of many social networking Web sites. There are special social media sites for kids, too. A parent or a trusted adult might show you pictures or posts from a social networking site for adults.

If you want to join a social networking site, ask your family for permission. An adult should help you get started, too.

People love sharing photos and videos on the Internet.

Ask if you are allowed to use any social media sites. Here are some rules to help keep you safe:

1. Your parents or a trusted adult should know what site you are on.
2. Never respond to a stranger online. Tell an adult if a stranger talks to you.
3. Don't share photos or videos without permission.
4. Tell an adult at once if anything you find online makes you worried.

Your family might have books of photos. Or maybe your family keeps your photo albums online. They post photos for friends and family to view. These photo album sites are private. Only people who know the password can see these sites.

A blog is a diary that is kept online. Blogs are mostly for adults. There are blogs on almost every topic. Some people blog about their hobbies. A bird-watcher might blog about the birds he or she sees. Other bird-watchers might enjoy reading that blog. You can even write a blog of your own! Ask an adult for help setting up a blog. Have an adult read what you write before you post it.

The Internet is a great way to share your life with others. But remember that anything you post online is there forever. And *everyone* can see it. Someone could read what you wrote or see your pictures years from now. So think twice before you post or upload.

Don't put information online that tells strangers
who you are or where you live.

Never put personal information on the Internet. Don't use your full name in an e-mail address. Use your first name or a nickname if you like. Or just make something up. Personal information includes these things:

- home address
- telephone number
- birth date
- last name
- passwords
- when your family will not be home
- where or when your parents work
- what school you go to
- where you are at the moment
- a description of yourself or things you like to do
- pictures of yourself
- anything about money

Never give personal information about anyone else on the Internet. You want to keep your friends and family safe, too. Ask an adult if you have any questions about something you see or something you want to post.

CHAPTER 4

Caution!

The Internet is the gateway to amazing worlds. It is a powerful tool for discovering new things. It builds connections between people. The Internet can make your life much better. But you need to be careful how you use it.

You've heard it before—don't talk to strangers. This applies to strangers on the Internet, too. People on the Internet might not be who they say they are. Never answer a message or e-mail from someone you don't know. Don't answer if a stranger asks questions about you or your family.

You might come across something you should not see even if you use a kid-friendly search engine. Tell an adult and close the browser window if you accidently see something wrong or bad. Your search engine might warn you if it is not safe to open a Web site. Do not open these sites. They could give your computer a virus.

Bullying can happen by e-mail, chat, social networking, or text.

You know what a bully is. A bully might say rude things about you. A bully might push you or trip you. A bully might try to make you do something you don't want to do. Cyberbullying is bullying online.

Cyberbullies can be hard to stop. They can hide behind a screen name. You might not know exactly who the cyberbully is. It can be one person or a group of people. Some people might think leaving someone out or ganging up on someone is fun. But if it hurts someone's feelings, it is bullying. Show an adult what the cyberbully did if someone bullies you. Do not respond to the message.

You need a password to get into many Web sites. Make a different password for each Web site. Make up passwords that are hard to crack. Do not use family or pet names. Use numbers and uppercase and lowercase letters. Use at least seven numbers or letters. Write your passwords down and keep them in a safe place away from the computer. Do not tell your passwords to your friends. Never give out your password on the Internet.

Does your family spend more time online than talking together? Try unplugging for a while.

Always be careful on the Internet. The best thing to do if you find something strange is to tell an adult. The Internet is an amazing tool, but remember that old saying: Safety first!

The Internet is a great place to play. But it is best not to spend too long there. Kids and teens spend from five to 44 hours a week surfing the Web. Your family should have rules about using the Internet. Those rules should include how much time you spend. Fifteen to 30 minutes at a time is enough. The computer you use should be in a room where your family spends time. That way your parents can check how long you are online.

Fingers and thumbs get a workout when you use the Internet. But remember to exercise the rest of your body, too. Go outside and walk or run. Jump and stretch when you are inside. Did you know that exercise helps your brain work better?

Don't forget that life happens in real time and space. Smile and talk to your friends and family. Play board games. Play outside. Help around the house. Remember the Internet is only one tool to help you learn and have fun. Enjoy using the Internet as one part of your full, fun life.

Enjoy time when you are not online, too!

TOP TEN THINGS TO KNOW

1. Use a kid-friendly search engine to look things up.
2. A reliable source usually has the author's name, a date, and links to other reliable Web sites.
3. Do not share personal information or photos online. Whatever you post on the Internet stays there forever.
4. Chat and enjoy social media, but only with friends and family.
5. Copying things on the Internet that should be paid for is the same as stealing them.
6. Never talk to strangers online.
7. If you have a question or something online upsets you, tell a trusted adult.
8. Tell an adult if you're being bullied online.
9. Make your passwords difficult to guess and keep them in a safe place.
10. Get off the Internet and play outside or meet up with your friends in real life.

GLOSSARY

communicate (kuh-MYOO-ni-kate) To communicate is to pass information from one person to another. We use the Internet to communicate with other people near and far.

convince (kuhn-VINS) To convince is to argue or show evidence to get someone to agree. Some Web sites may try to convince people of something that isn't true.

encyclopedia (en-sye-klo-PEE-dee-uh) An encyclopedia is a work that contains information on all subjects arranged alphabetically. An encyclopedia can be online or it can be one or more books.

hacked (HAKD) Something that has been hacked has been broken into online. If your password is easy to guess, your account might be hacked.

opinion (uh-PIN-yuhn) An opinion is a judgment about someone or something. Many Web sites have someone's opinion rather than plain facts.

plagiarism (PLAY-juh-rih-sem) Plagiarism is taking another person's words or ideas and using them as if they were yours. Plagiarism is a type of stealing.

search engine (SURCH EN-jin) A search engine is an online program that searches the Internet for information. Use a search engine to find music and movies online, too.

social networking site (SOH-shul NET-wur-king SITE) A social networking site is an online group or community people join. Another term for social networking is social media.

spam (SPAM) Spam is e-mail, usually from a business, that is sent to a large number of people. Delete spam e-mail and don't open it.

virus (VYE-ruhs) A virus is a computer program that can cause damage. A virus can be hidden in an e-mail or accidentally downloaded by clicking a link.

BOOKS

Buzzeo, Toni. *But I Read It on the Internet!* Madison, WI: Upstart Books, 2013.

Goldsmith, Mike, and Tom Jackson. *Computer*. New York: DK Publishing, 2011.

Yomtov, Nelson. *Internet Inventors.* New York: Children's Press, 2013.

WEB SITES

Visit our Web site for links about using the Internet:
childsworld.com/links

Note to Parents, Teachers, and Librarians:
We routinely verify our Web links to make sure they are safe and active sites. So encourage your readers to check them out!

INDEX